Lilian Tomu

Short Sketch Of The Life Of Sergeant Major J. I. Nunnerley, Late of the Lancashire Hussars

Lilian Tomu

Short Sketch Of The Life Of Sergeant Major J. I. Nunnerley, Late of the Lancashire Hussars

ISBN/EAN: 9783742891693

Manufactured in Europe, USA, Canada, Australia, Japa

Cover: Foto ©ninafisch / pixelio.de

Manufactured and distributed by brebook publishing software (www.brebook.com)

Lilian Tomu

Short Sketch Of The Life Of Sergeant Major J. I. Nunnerley, Late of the Lancashire Hussars

SERGEANT-MAJOR J. I. NUNNERLEY,

One of the "Six hundred."

SHORT SKETCH

OF THE

LIFE

OF

SERGEANT-MAJOR J. I. NUNNERLEY,

LATE OF THE LANCASHIRE HUSSARS,

AND FORMERLY

SERGEANT OF THE "DEATH OR GLORY BOYS"

(17TH LANCERS),

AND

One of the "Six Hundred."

ORMSKIRK:
PRINTED BY P. DRAPER, 12, BURSCOUGH-STREET.

1890.

SHORT SKETCH

OF THE

LIFE

OF

SERGEANT-MAJOR NUNNERLEY.

"A genial, kindly, modest Englishman,
And also a brave soldier.   One who rode
The ever-famous charge at Balaklava
With the "Six Hundred," whom to name or think of
Sets the heart leaping like the sound of trumpet,
Moistens the eye, and makes the voice to falter ;
And shall do so while England is a nation
(If it please God, for ages.)"

BIRTH AND PARENTAGE.

THE subject of this sketch was born at Wilderspool, in Cheshire; and was the seventh son of Richard Nunnerley, who died in 1870, at the advanced age of eighty years.   Richard Nunnerley was a native of Shropshire, and served in the yeomanry cavalry of that county for a considerable time, but afterwards resided near Warrington. He was a descendant of John Nunnerley, who, more than a century and a half ago, lived at Tetchel Moor, Salop, where he was in possession of a moderate competency.   It was to our gallant hero's paternal grandmother, Ann Jebb, of Whixall, Salop, that the valentines (copies of which are appended) were addressed, and which, in the year 1873, were extracted from the Journal of the British Archæological Association, and exhibited by Dr. Kendrick, of Warrington.   Lieutenant George Jebb died abroad of yellow fever, in 1800, whilst serving in the British Army. Lieutenant Wright John Jebb served in the North Shropshire Yeomanry for thirty-eight years, and retired in 1836.   These were brothers to Ann Jebb.

Sergeant-Major Nunnerley's mother was the daughter of William Ikin, of Nantwich, Cheshire, where he carried on the business of timber merchant and builder for fifty-five years, and died in the year 1841, at the ripe age of seventy-five years. Peace being proclaimed in the year 1815, after the long Peninsular War, which was closed by the famous battle of Waterloo, the occasion was honoured in Nantwich Church in the shape of a magnificent blind or screen for the west window, on which were painted representations of the three Christian Graces, "Faith, Hope, and Charity." The future mother of Sergeant-Major Nunnerley was then about twenty-two years of age, and being considered the prettiest of the gentle sex of the town, she was selected to pourtray the centre figure in the group—"Hope." She was married in the year 1819, at Knutsford, and became the mother of nine children, the first eight being sons, and the last child a daughter. The subject of this narrative was the seventh son. Of his seven brothers, two joined the Army, and received medals; a third entered the Navy; and some of the others enrolled themselves as Volunteers. The sixth son, Wright Jebb Nunnerley, was second-class officer on board ship in the years 1852-3-4; and, during the Burmese War, took part in the taking of a fort at Pegu, for which he received a medal and a considerable amount of prize-money. The youngest son served in the Horse Artillery as sergeant, and was engaged in the Crimean War; and, for his services, is in possession of the "English Medal," with one clasp, together with the "Turkish Medal." Wright Jebb Nunnerley was the father of Philip Jebb Nunnerley, who, in 1887, served in the British Army as captain and doctor in the War in Upper Burmah, and received the Medal for it.

Before commencing to notice the military career of Sergeant-Major Nunnerley, a slight digression may not be deemed wholly uninteresting. The uncle of Sergeant-Major Nunnerley was the father of Miss Nunnerley, whose death and remarkable funeral formed the subjects and eloquent lesson of the following paragraph, which appeared in the public newspapers at the time of the sad and painful event:—"An extraordinary funeral took place at Whitchurch a few days ago, Miss Nunnerley, of Wirswall, Cheshire, being interred in all her wedding clothes, even to the wreath, boots, and ring. The young lady was engaged to be married to a cheese factor from London, a son of Mr. R. W. Burgess, cheese factor, Whitchurch. The wedding was postponed owing to the illness of the young lady's father, who died six weeks ago, the day after the ceremony was fixed. As, however, all the preparations for the wedding had been made, it was decided for it to take place quietly some three weeks ago, but a day or so before the date, Miss Nunnerley herself was taken ill, and died. 'In the midst of life we are in death;' and in all cases it is better to 'set our affections on things above,' for then only are we sure of sustaining no disappointment. He who betroths us unto Himself dies not, and His bride has an inheritance of immortality in Him."—This Miss Sarah Nunnerley was the daughter of John Nunnerley, who died at Wirswall, Cheshire, on the 18th of September, 1884, aged 77 years; and his beloved and affectionate daughter, the said Sarah Nunnerley, also died at Wirswall, on the 3rd of November, 1884, aged 23 years.

> "Not gone from memory, not gone from love,
> But gone to their Father's home above."

As already observed, the parents of Sergeant-Major Nunnerley, with their large family, took up their residence at Wilderspool, near Warrington; and in 1843 the mother died. At the early age of twelve years, the subject of our sketch was instrumental in saving the life of a companion. Two boys, named John and William Mason, with young James Ikin Nunnerley, were in a rowing boat on the Duke's Canal, near Warrington, when John Mason would get out of the boat as a flat was passing. He got on the side of the boat to spring on to the flat, when the boat was turned upside down, with Nunnerley and William Mason underneath it. Nunnerley rescued William Mason from under the boat and swam with him and landed him safely on the bank. In 1844, the future Sergeant-Major was apprenticed to a draper at Warrington; but, having had from his earliest days a very strong and growing inclination for a soldier's life, he rapidly developed his decision to join the Army, and began to cogitate as to which of the cavalry regiments he should elect to attach himself. At the expiration of a fortnight, his preference gravitated towards the 17th Lancers, and he at once acquainted his father and friends of his determination to join that regiment. His friends, as might be expected under the circumstances, tried all their persuasive powers to dispel the idea from the ardent embryo soldier; but, finding his determination was not to be thwarted, and their persuasions of no avail, his relatives yielded to his young and indomitable will.

JOINING THE ARMY.

It was in the year 1846 that, having taken leave of his relatives and friends, he proceeded to Liverpool, accompanied by his father, who saw him on "board ship," bound for Dundalk, Ireland, where the 17th Lancers were stationed, and at which place he was now destined to commence his military career. He remained in Ireland with his regiment until the year 1851. During his stay in Ireland, his regiment, with 16,000 of the line, was reviewed by the Queen and the Prince Consort in Phœnix Park, Dublin. While stationed in Dublin, in the year 1848, the 17th Lancers were on duty day and night engaged in quelling the "Rebellion of Smith O'Brien," then member for

Limerick, who was at that time giving the Government considerable anxiety and trouble.

In 1851, having been ordered to England, the regiment landed at Liverpool, and proceeded to London, and thence marched to Woolwich, where it took up its quarters. Sometime after, the regiment proceeded to Hampton Court and Hounslow, where it received orders for the Crimea.

At the funeral of the illustrious Duke of Wellington, young Nunnerley, who had then gained the rank of corporal, took his part as such with the dismounted party, there being one sergeant, one corporal, and twelve men picked out of every regiment in the service, commanded by an officer.

THE CRIMEAN WAR.

In 1854, England and France declared war against Russia, which Power, having destroyed the Turkish Fleet, manifested her intention to dismember Turkey itself after the "bag and baggage" fashion. Detachments of the British army, including the 17th Lancers, were therefore "ordered out" for Turkey to the aid of the Turks. Landing at Coolalee, opposite Constantinople, the 17th Lancers remained there for a week, for the purpose of refreshing their horses and men. They then embarked for Varna, a town on the east coast of Turkey, and situated on the Black Sea. When nearing Varna, young Nunnerley had the misfortune to fall overboard; but, luckily, he had learned to swim, and, after battling with the waves for some time, he was rescued by a small boat, and put on board again. They disembarked the same day, and had to sleep all night on the ground, with their clothes on, the only other covering afforded them being a blanket. After staying a few days at Varna, they "formed" and marched to Yeni Bazar, and thence to Devna, towards Silistria, headed by the brave Lord Cardigan, who, at the former place, had the Light Cavalry in line for the inspection of Omar Pasha, who, mounted on a splendid Arab charger, put the regiment through several movements, especially that of charging in line, in which the reviewing officer was left far behind. The dash and efficiency of the men called forth Omar Pasha's admiration, and led him to exclaim, as with a prophetic prescience of the forthcoming struggles, "Nothing in the world could stand against the English Cavalry!"

> "A cheer, a loud and hearty cheer!
> A welcome to the heroes here,
> Who by their deeds, through every age
> Will foremost stand in history's page."

Whilst in Turkey, the 17th Lancers lost a great many men through the prevalence of cholera and dysentery, which, sweeping through the ranks, made terrible havoc of them. Lance-Sergeant Brennan, after the march, partook very freely of the fruit of a plum-tree, up which he had climbed. This brought on the cholera, and, before night, the regiment had lost a good and faithful man.

Young Nunnerley being one of the best in health, the duty of gravedigger often fell upon him, both in Turkey and in the Crimea. But he, in his turn, was taken sick. Whilst on the road returning to Varna, he had an attack of fever, and was ordered by the doctor to the Scutaria Hospital. At his earnest request however, he was allowed to embark with the regiment for the Crimea, on condition that he would not land unless his recovery was complete. Upon his arrival, his health was completely restored, and he landed with his regiment at Eupatoria, on the 17th September, 1854, and, on the following day, marched towards Sebastopol. After having picketed the horses, a search for forage took place. Upon crossing a small tract of land, with the two men allowed him, they fortunately came across a hole near a house, upon which sods and grass had been laid by the Russians so as to deceive their enemy. On taking off the sods, they found the hole contained eighteen sacks of good barley. They at once took possession of this, which supplied the requirements of the regiment, and left a considerable quantity for distribution amongst the other regiments. During their night's repose on the ground, they were visited by a tremendous shower of musket bullets, which came whistling through their lines, doing no damage, however, owing to having been fired too high. In a few minutes they were on their horses, but not one of the Russians could be seen.

On the 19th September, the British proceeded in the order of battle to Bulganack, and, when nearly at the end of their march, just as darkness had overtaken them, some of the men were picking up melons with their lances, when a number of Cossacks, who were thrown out in skirmishing order, came galloping in front of their infantry and commenced an engagement. They were soon compelled to retreat, our Horse Artillery playing upon them very effectively, and unlimbering one of their guns. The loss of the Cossacks was very considerable, as they were a very long time fully occupied in carrying their dead and wounded off the field. The loss of the Light Cavalry was very slight, but three men had their feet blown off, the result of the low firing of the enemy, and about nine horses killed. The loss would have proved much more serious had not Colonel Lawrenson, who commanded the 17th Lancers, wheeled the troops to the left just in time to escape the deadly cannon-shot of the enemy, which swept through the intervals.

THE BATTLE OF ALMA.

On the 20th of September, the British Army, together with their allies—the French and Turks—left Bulganack and again marched on the road in the order of battle, frequently coming across large numbers of dead horses, which had been wounded in the sharp engagement of the previous day, and had died on the road. After a day's march, our progress was checked by the enemy. The Russians had posted themselves on the south side of the Alma, which position the Russian General said he could hold for six weeks against any force brought against it. So confident was he in the impregnability of his position and the discipline and strength of the forces who held it, that, coupled with the confidence of his assertion, gentlemen's carriages were so placed that the occupants might witness the engagement which was now inevitable. The British Infantry, who were on the left, were the first to commence action, and upon them the heat of the battle fell : the Turks were next in order ; and the French maintained the position on the right, near the sea. Right bravely they [fought, facing other difficulties as well as the foe, but undaunted by either. Dashing through the river, they kept up the attack on the enemy with the utmost vigour and persistency ; but, against such odds and difficulties, they were obliged temporarily to retrace their steps for fresh ammunition, as in some places, where the river was deep, their supply got wet, and was thus rendered useless. However, their delay on this account was but short, and, rushing into the river, they again faced their foe. In consequence of the French being very much behind, they found it desirable to come to a standstill. They were now about 100 yards from the line of the enemy's fire, and, as every shot was proving disastrous, the French came up and formed in line. The British Infantry then charged the enemy, who quickly retired from their position, and were repulsed with a heavy loss. Thus the Alma, which, from the statement of the Russian commander, was not to be taken within six weeks, was now carried and captured within two hours and a half from the commencement of the engagement. The carriages, about whose safety the Russian general had been so sanguine !— Where were they ? Some of the occupants were made alive to their critical position at the commencement of the struggle, and had left the field, and could be seen making their escape as fast as possible towards Sebastopol. Others only became aware of their perilous position when it was too late. The British Cavalry, which was only a quarter the strength of that of the enemy, protected their left flank. Had it been otherwise, the loss of the Allies would have been much heavier, as the Russian Cavalry, about 2,000 strong, were seen going through some strategic movements, endeavouring to get round the left flank of the British. Finding their efforts vain, and our troops advancing, the Russians galloped away, not daring to encounter them. The squadron of the 17th Lancers, to which young Nunnerley belonged, was then sent in pursuit of the enemy, when, while on their ghastly errand, sights better imagined than described met their eyes ! The dead and the dying were lying so thickly on the ground that they could with difficulty keep their horses from treading upon them. Eventually, they overtook the enemy, who soon fell upon their knees, and, giving up their arms, were made prisoners.

In this desperate battle, being the first in the campaign, the Russians lost 5,700 killed and wounded, and about 2,300 were made prisoners. The loss of the British was 2,500 killed and wounded, their Allies losing only 500 killed and wounded. The Navy rendered great assistance, their guns, issuing forth destructive shells, made great slaughter, one shell killing sixteen men, besides wounding many others. The British Infantry captured two brass cannons from the Russians in this engagement.

The Battle of Alma closes with the following incidents :—After the engagement, two of the 60th Rifles went across the Alma Hills for water, which having been obtained, when returning, they saw two wounded Russians lying on the ground. Although they were foes, the humanity of the two Rifles led them to offer the poor fellows some water, which was readily accepted. In return for this kindness, one of these wounded Russians, as the two Rifles were leaving, levelled his musket, and shot one of the two Rifles. This ungrateful treachery so filled the other comrade Rifle with disgust, that he immediately ran back to the Russian who had perpetrated the foul deed, and, taking the musket out of his hand, dashed out his brains with the butt end, a fate he richly deserved. The same day, Nunnerley and his comrades witnessed the fidelity and affection which a little fox-terrier had for its master, a Russian, who lay dead on the field—one of the sixteen Russians killed by the before-mentioned shell. The faithful little animal, with all tenderness and pitifulness, lay between its master's legs, not allowing anyone to touch him ; and the consternation which it created amongst the brave British soldiers, who seemed afraid of being bitten, caused no little amusement.

Just before darkness set in, after having drawn the dead and dying out of the lines, our Cavalry proceeded to picket their horses. Both men and horses were suffering most severely from thirst, and it was necessary to take the horses to the river for water. The sight there was one that never could be forgotten by those who witnessed it :—a river reddened with blood, and man and beast alike eagerly and gratefully drinking of its blood-stained waters ! They afterwards prepared for the night's rest on Alma Hill, where they lay amongst the dead and dying, and were partially stifled with the dreadful odours arising from so many unburied bodies. The next day they commenced the sad task of burying the dead, which took more than two days to accomplish. During the time indescribable sights, which struck the stoutest with awe, met their gaze. Some dead, others on the point of death, many having bullet wounds in their heads, bleeding freely.

WHAT will they say in England?
When the story there is told
Of deeds of might, on Alma's Heights,
Done by the brave and bold?
Of Russia, proud at noontide,
Humbled ere set of sun?
They'll say 'twas like old England;
They'll say 'twas nobly done!

What will they say in England?
When hushed in awe and dread,
Fond hearts through all our happy homes
Think of the mighty dead;
And muse in speechless anguish,
On Father, Brother, Son,
They'll say in Christian England,
God's holy will be done.

What will they say in England?
The Matron and the Maid,
Whose widow'd withered hearts have found
The price that each has paid;
The gladness that their homes have lost
For all the glory won.
They'll say in Christian England,
God's holy will be done.

What will they say in England?
Our names both night and day
Are on their lips, and in their hearts,
When they laugh, or weep, or pray;
They watch on earth, they plead with heaven,
Then forward to the fight.
Who dreads or fears when England cheers,
And God defends the right!

On the 25th of September, after having completed the solemn task of burying the dead, the British concealed themselves in a jungle, near Mc.Kenzie's Farm, whence, upon emerging therefrom, they found the enemy had disappeared. Riding quickly in pursuit, after a good gallop of two miles, they were overtaken. The Horse Artillery, having unlimbered their guns, fired upon them, completely overturning their baggage-waggons and carts. The British afterwards took possession of their ammunition waggons, together with a van containing the pay for the whole of the Russian army in and around Sebastopol, as well as other important valuables.

The following day, a fort, called Balaklava, whose harbour it defended, was captured; and, on the 11th October following, the Allies had another skirmish with the Russians.

THE CHARGE OF THE LIGHT BRIGADE.

The 25th October brought about that dreadful doom to the regiment to which Sergeant-Major Nunnerley's fortunes and warlike experiences were involved; and upon which so many writers, in prose and verse, at various times have commented, and rendered famous in "history's story." This terrible engagement commenced by the Russians attacking a fort commanded by the Turks, who made a stout resistance for a considerable time; but, being outnumbered, were compelled to retire, after which the British Heavy Cavalry advanced to cover their retreat. The Russian Cavalry afterwards came down upon our Infantry, which consisted of the 93rd regiment and Two Turkish regiments, the latter being placed on each flank of the 93rd, all in line. When the enemy was within two hundred yards, the Turks ran away, and left the 93rd, who stood their ground, like "a stone wall," to face the enemy. They immediately opened a heavy fire into the Russian Cavalry, causing them quickly to retreat. Finding themselves foiled in this attack on the Infantry, the Russians changed their position, and approached our Heavy Cavalry, whose strength was only one-fourth of their's. Our Heavy Cavalry waited until the Russian Cavalry were within one hundred yards, when, without regarding numbers, they charged and dashed right through the Russian line, cutting their way back in splendid style. The Russian Cavalry then retreated behind the hills, near to their Infantry, who where 20,000 strong, and were formed in solid squares, besides having 14 guns so placed as to command the long valley these hills inclosed, and since known as the "Valley of Death." The Russian Cavalry, having retreated, were placed under both hills, facing inwards, a little in advance of the guns. But now came the extraordinary charge, so well known as the "Charge of the Light Brigade," or the "Charge of the Six Hundred," the blundering of which proved so disastrous, and appears so conspicuous in history. The Light Brigade of Cavalry was formed; and, although a mere handful in comparison with the enemy, were commanded to charge the Russian guns and an army of about 22,000 men. Headed by Lord Cardigan, our Light Brigade advanced against their formidable foes, and were met with a regular cross fire of shot and shell from the guns on the side hills and from those at the entrance to the valley, sweeping them down in all directions, and making terrible havoc amongst them. Still the Light Brigade advanced, and, charging the guns, took them, but could not hold them, as the Russian Cavalry, wheeling right and left, surrounded our Light Brigade, and entirely blocked them in. This was a critical moment! The gallant Light Brigade, nothing daunted, formed themselves into small bodies, and charged—as none but British can charge—right through the Russian Cavalry back again. This was indeed a struggle for country and honour; and will ever rank amongst the bravest and bloodiest engagements portraying the exploits, dash and daring of the British Cavalry!

The following is the personal narrative of Sergeant-Major Nunnerley :—Whilst charging the guns, he was in the first line of the right squadron of his regiment.   He saw Captain Nolan ride up to Lord Cardigan, who was in front of the left squadron, and, after giving his Lordship the order, ride up to Captain Morris, then commanding the 17th Lancers, to whom he said, "Now, Morris, for a bit of fun!"   Scarcely had he uttered these words than he was shot, being at the time on Sergeant-Major Nunnerley's left front.   After giving a kind of yell, which sounded very much like "Threes right," and throwing his sword-hand above his head, his horse wheeled to the right, and he fell to the rear.   As though obeying this death-like order, part of the squadron wheeled "Threes right," and, observing their left squadron advancing, with Lord Cardigan in front, Sergeant-Major Nunnerley immediately gave the order "Front, forward!" and so brought them into line again.   They had not proceeded far before the men in the left division of his squadron were nearly all cut down, including a sergeant, who had his head blown off, but afterwards rode about thirty yards before he fell.   Every shot from the enemy's guns now came with the most deadly accuracy; and he (Sergeant-Major Nunnerley) was not without his "hairbreadth escapes," for when he was within a few yards of the Russian guns, his horse was shot under him and fell on its head.   He endeavoured to pull it up in order to dash at the gunners, but found it was unable to move, its foreleg having been blown off.   He then left it and forced his way on foot through shot and shell, when he was attacked by the Russian Cavalry, through whom he cut his way, his more than ordinary height, combined with a powerful frame, proving at this crisis most advantageous to him.   He had no sooner got clear of his foes than he was knocked down and ridden over by a number of riderless horses, together with a few Hussars.   Having regained his feet, he observed one of the 13th Light Dragoons under his horse, which had been killed, the rider not being able to free himself.   He dragged the horse off him, and set him at liberty, and accompanied him a short distance till he fell in with Sergeant John Farrell of his own regiment.   He assisted Farrell to carry Captain Webb out of danger on a stretcher, which had been brought to their aid by Sergeant John Berryman.   He then returned under a heavy fire to the field, and brought out Trumpeter William Britton, who was very seriously wounded; and, after having obtained water for him and the remainder of the wounded, he caught a horse belonging to the 8th Hussars, whose rider had been shot, which he mounted, and then joined his regiment.   After this came the painful task of numbering of.   He found that out of the 145 belonging to the regiment who went into the charge only 35 could be found,—the result of this terrible charge of about half-an-hour's duration!   Some were on Russian horses, and others on horses belonging to other regiments, whose riders had been killed.   Before this battle commenced, there were

13 men in his tent, but after the charge, he was the only one left. Had not this charge been made, his opinion is, that they would have lost Balaklava Harbour, as he firmly believes that the Russians intended retaking it. During the charge, the Turks, who ran away at the commencement of the engagement, entered the British tents, and consumed or took away all the provisions they could find therein. Such was the honour of the men for whose rights the British were fighting!

CHARGE OF THE LIGHT BRIGADE.

HALF a league, half a league,
   Half a league onward,
All in the valley of Death
   Rode the six hundred.
"Forward, the Light Brigade!
Charge for the guns!" he said:
Into the valley of Death
   Rode the six hundred.

"Forward, the Light Brigade!"
Was there a man dismayed?
Not, tho' the soldier knew
   Some one had blunder'd:
Theirs not to make reply,
Theirs not to reason why,
Theirs but to do and die,
Into the valley of Death
   Rode the six hundred.

Cannon to right of them,
Cannon to left of them,
Cannon in front of them
   Volley'd and thundered;
Storm'd at with shot and shell,
Boldly they rode and well,
Into the jaws of Death,
Into the mouth of Hell
   Rode the six hundred.

Flash'd all their sabres bare,
Flash'd as they turn'd in air,
Sabring the gunners there,
Charging an army, while
   All the world wonder'd:
Plunged in the battery smoke
Right through the line they broke
Cossack and Russian
Reel'd from the sabre-stroke
   Shatter'd and sundered.
Then they rode back, but not,
Not the six hundred.

Cannon to right of them,
Cannon to left of them,
Cannon behind them
   Volley'd and thunder'd;
Storm'd at with shot and shell,
While horse and hero fell,
They that had fought so well
Came through the jaws of Death
Back from the mouth of Hell,
All that was left of them,
   Left of six hundred.

When can their glory fade;
O the wild charge they made!
   All the world wonder'd.
Honour the charge they made!
Honour the Light Brigade,
   Noble six hundred!

To the Memory of the Noble Leader,
LORD CARDIGAN.

RISE, Comrades! lift the gleaming glass,
   Gay laughter now is fled,
In solemn silence we will drink
"The memory of our Dead!"
And first we pledge the hero's name,
Who in the Death Charge led!

This day the present from us glides,
The glorious past draws near;

Our own proud joy of triumph blends
With sorrow's starting tear,
And high upon our roll of fame,
Let " Cardigan " appear.

We think upon his burning wish
On the Crimean strand—
That we might be the first to meet
The hostile Russian's band !
And first we were, with keen drawn swords
In foeman's front to stand !

And still he chafed to lead us on,
Until the fated day,
When down that Northern Vale we rode,
Fought Death, and tore away !
And show'd the world what soldiers mean
By that short word—" Obey ! "

'Twas priceless, in that hour supreme,
That we our Leader knew ;
We knew the love of flashing steel
Glanced in his eyes so blue,
And though his word was strict and stern,
His heart was strong and true.

We honour'd him, as soldiers love
A firm and dauntless man ;
We knew he prized our valour well,
As but a brave man can :
And freely gave we in return,
Our trust to Cardigan !

He rode in front of all our line,
First horse and foremost blade ;
And generous hearts lay lighter stress
When a brave man's faults are weighed ;
These words form his immortal wreath—
" He led the Light Brigade ! "

It has been asserted by some who have written descriptions of
the "Charge of the Light Brigade," that Lord Cardigan was not
in the Charge. Sergeant-Major Nunnerley, however, positively
asserts that he saw his Lordship in front of the left squadron of
the 17th Lancers, who were with the 13th Light Dragoons, in the
front line ; and, after the Charge, he again saw his Lordship,
as he was giving orders to the remnant of the "Six Hundred" to
form, near the spot whence they started for the Charge.

THE LIGHT BRIGADE.

HAIL, Comrades of the fearful fight
    On Balaklava's bloody day !
With solemn, but with proud delight,
    We meet in memory of that fray ;
A bitter fray it was to all
    Who in our " *Charge* " the hero play'd ;
And foes and friends it did appal,
    Yet crowned with fame "*the Light Brigade.*"

Who shall forget the cannons' roar—
   The clash—the shout—the wild *mêlée*—
The sad retreat—when we no more
   'Gainst frightful odds could aught essay?
While War continues to enlarge,
   And History's sanguine page degrade,
Will live "*The Balaklava Charge,*"
   And England's glorious "*Light Brigade.*"

Few answered to the muster call
   When the disastrous fight was done;
Marvel not, then, our muster's small,
   When one-and-twenty years have gone!
Still, while of "*the Six Hundred*" yet
   But *one* is left on life's parade,
He never—never will forget
   His comrades of "*the Light Brigade.*"

Then charge your glasses! Comrades, fill!—
   When duty calls, we must obey:
Honour each soldier's breast should thrill,
   And death be powerless to dismay!
Long may our *Navy* be supreme—
   Nothing our *Army* e'er degrade;
And "THE SIX HUNDRED" be the theme
   To cheer some future "LIGHT BRIGADE!"

INKERMAN.

On the 5th of November, 1854, a day observed in England for the discharging of miniature cannons and the lighting of bonfires, the British were attacked by the enemy at Inkerman; and it *was* a fifth of November in reality, which the men could not help remarking. In this engagement our loss was considerable, but the loss was ten times greater to the enemy, who had been repulsed by our Foot Guards and Light Infantry three times. At this juncture, the Foot Guards found themselves short of ammunition, but, instead of being baffled by this difficulty, they immediately made free use of the stones and other missiles lying around, with which they kept up a continuous fusilade on the enemy until relieved by 6,000 French, who arrived with fresh ammunition, and gave the enemy the benefit of it, as they were in full retreat. The 17th Lancers were posted in a hollow during this engagement, ready for any emergency, in case the line of Guards was broken. This position they found a very critical one, and far worse than being actually engaged, as the shot from the enemy's cannon continually fell behind the Guards, and then rebounded over their heads. To escape this, they had to be continually on the watch. Some, however, were not fortunate enough to escape from the shells, and Sergeant-Major Nunnerley, like many others, had several very narrow escapes, one of which he describes as follows:—A shell from the Russian shipping fell in front of them, and penetrated the ground about three feet, after which it exploded, tearing up everything round about it, and wounding Cornet Cleveland, (the officer in front of Sergeant-Major Nunnerley), who died the next day, and was buried by our gallant soldiers underneath a stone wall, about one hundred yards from the place where he fell. The shell also killed the man next but one on his left, deprived the man on his right of the left arm, knocked about nine horses down ; but, fortunately, left Sergeant-Major Nunnerley and his horse uninjured.

Whilst the Light Brigade were in camp at Inkerman, after the battle, they were very short of water and forage for the horses. The coffee was served out unroasted, and the biscuits were mouldy. Not being able to get either water or firewood, they could not get anything warm, and had to eat the mouldy biscuits to raw salt pork and beef, which was the cause of so much scurvy amongst the men. Many got frost-bitten through not having shoes or boots, which caused their toes to drop off. The river Technia ran betwixt them and the Russians, which made it rather awkward to obtain water, as the Russians fired on them.—Of course they returned the compliment whilst the Russians were getting their water. It was very hard for the men without boots, as every time they went out of the tent they were up to their ankles in mud. It was also very pitiful to see the horses with little or no forage—some dropping down dead in the lines through starvation. The horses would often slip their ropes and eat the manes and tails of each other, as well as those of the dead horses. To get water, they used to tie up the bottom of their tents when it rained to catch the falling water ; at other times they used snow or ice, or water laden out of the holes made by the horses' feet. When ordered from Inkerman to Balaklava, they had very few horses left, and these so weak that they could not carry a man, many lying down on the road, where they were left to die.

On the 14th of November, just before they left Inkerman, a tremendous storm took place, which caused the loss of about 14 ships laden with clothes, &c., for the use of the Army. The wife of one of the 17th Lancers was on one of them, and the next day her husband went to look for her corpse on the shore, as he knew she had some bank notes stitched in her stays. After a search of an hour, he found her, naked, except her stays, and, to his great surprise, the notes were safe. A private of the same regiment on picket in front of the enemy, left his post to get a drink at Balaklava. He got rather too much, and, in returning, fell off his horse, and afterwards scrambled into a cooking-shed belonging to the Turks, and lay down near the door, where he fell asleep. During the night it rained very hard and flooded the place where he lay. The Turks, who were cooking, passed him every minute, but would not pull him out, although he lay on his side with only his head and arms out of water. If some of the Lancers had not found him, the Turks would have left him there to drown or die.

During the time they were in tents on Balaklava Hill, in the winter of 1854, the tents were so far worn that the rain came through. When this happened, they made a gutter from the top of the tent to the bottom, so that the water could run at the door ; and for amusement they made paper boats and had races, the "boat" out of doors first was the winner. When night came they had to lie down on the same place. At Balaklava they had a cook, named Stoddard, whose feet were frost-bitten ; and, when frost-bitten, the feet are quite numb. He shewed them his feet, and took hold of his toes one after the other, and, to our surprise, they came off at the first joint. He held them up separately, saying "I am only a piece of a man now," and threw them away.

At the battle of the Alma, a spent bullet struck a private, of the name of George Dunn, in the back ; but, having a cholera belt on, it turned the bullet so that it went round inside his trouser's waist to the front. On putting his hand there, he drew the bullet out, thinking it had gone through him, but he was not hurt.

After the railway was complete from Balaklava to Sebastopol, it was of very good service in getting shot and shell up to the front. Had it not been for this railway, Sebastopol would not have fallen so soon as it did. It was also useful in bringing the dead from the front to Balaklava, where holes were made about 7ft. wide, 10ft. long, and 5ft. deep. In these holes they placed about three layers of bodies, with soil, about a foot in depth, laid between each. This frequently occurred, for some fell daily, and especially during a sortie made by the Russians for the purpose of taking the trenches, an attempt that was altogether fruitless. Those who died through sickness were brought down, with the killed, in the railway waggons.

In August, 1855, they were sent to Baidor on the road to Simpheropol with the squadron in advance. Coming to a river they were on the point of watering their horses, when they were astonished at seeing several hundreds of cattle belonging to the army lying dead not far from its banks. The waters of the river had, by the treachery of the enemy, been poisoned, and to the cattle partaking thereof death was the result. The cattle lying there was a warning to them, and they refrained from allowing their horses to drink from this polluted stream.

In Memory of ARCHIBALD CLEVELAND, Esq., 17th Lancers,
of Tapley Park, North Devon, aged 21, who fell on the 5th
November, at the Battle of Inkerman, addressed to his bereaved
Mother.

DEEP in the foeman's mould he lies,
    The youthful and the brave ;
Without a stone to speak his worth,
    Or mark the soldier's grave.

A cry for help came o'er the seas,
    The Osmali to shield ;
He heard it, and with maiden sword
    He sought the battle field.

We bless'd him as he left his home
    His noble soul to prove ;
We lov'd him for our England's sake,
    And he returned our love.

We never doubted once his heart
    Was daring to a sin ;
We knew his patriotic fire,
    And mettle of his kin.

And, knowing him, our watchful love
    Pursued the path he trod ;
And, when his footprints mock'd our search,
    We left him to his God.

Grim death, with scythe of pestilence,
    Britannia's flower mowed down ;
We saw him mourn those hero-sons,
    Of England's old renown.

And bending with a wistful gaze
    To see his comrades die,
He heard those dying Britons say
    "Our country's loss supply."

With eye upturned to Heaven, he asked
    That he in peril's hour,
Rememb'ring how the brave could die,
    Might have their share of power.

His prayer was heard, his wish was seal'd,
    The hour immortal came,
And Balaklava wrote in blood
    The Lancer's deathless name.

The order came "Advance !"—enough,
    And veterans held their breath
To see our troopers plough through fire
    A pathway to their death.

To doubt if it were wisely given,
    Was not a hero's part :
But "Onward" like a lightning stream
    And scorch the foeman's heart.

One deed of daring such as that
    It takes an age to give ;
Such thought we had, and pray'd that Fate
    Would let the victor live.

We dwelt upon the matchless charge,
  And hop'd your darling pride
Would oft beguile, with martial tales
  Your hours at eventide.

But Freedom claim'd him for her own
  And Glory begged his name
Might be enroll'd among the great,
  A favourite of Fame.

So came the fight at Inkerman,
  Unparalleled by wars,
When England drove the savage foe
  As thick as midnight stars.

And there he fell, as falls the brave,
  Her right-true gallant son ;
One of those chosen souls who make
  The base of Freedom's Throne.

The thunder of that famous fray
  Broke loud upon the shore ;
And eagerly we sought the list
  Of those to fight no more.

It came too soon— our grief gush'd out
  In torrents unsubdued,
For first of all those glorious ones
  The name of " Cleveland " stood !

(A weeper once, in ancient days,
  Mourned where a Hebrew slept ;
The noblest soul on earth was He,
  But history says, " He wept.")

We wept, humanity must weep,
  So nature dropped a tear ;
Then pictured we his shroudless corpse
  Stretch'd on his grassy bier.

We saw a gentle comrade's hand
  Press lightly on his head ;
Then, with his fellow soldiers, make
  The warrior's narrow bed.

No manufactur'd pomp of Death
  Bedeck'd his coffin rude ;
His mourners were those bleeding hearts
  Which heaped the field of blood.

A carriage borrow'd from the war
  The hearse's office did ;
His cap upon the coffin rode,
  His sword across the lid.

No muffled drum, no funeral pall,
  Salute, nor solemn knell
Told how they sorrowed o'er their loss,
  But tears, and one farewell.

A little mound we saw them raise
  Upon that broken slope ;
Then weeping went to bind and soothe
  Our country's pride and hope.

C

Full many a kindred deed that day
  All piously was done ;
Whilst war rode out a requiem
  As gun replied to gun.

No floweret there may crown their graves
  As our sweet daisies do ;
But this our Fatherland hath sworn
  To wrench them from the foe.

Peace, Lady, thou hast done thy part—
  A son thou hadst to give ;
Now England writes his epitaph—
  " He died that I might live !"

On the 7th August, whilst stopping at Baidor, Sergeant-Major Nunnerley's regiment proceeded to Prince Worouzoft's residence, taking with them all the baggage-carts and waggons possible. Upon arriving, they found it untenanted, but in charge of a guard of Russian Infantry, who fired at them, slightly wounding two drivers and killing a mule, and then retired. After a thorough search and examination of this residence, they returned with the waggons laden with champagne and other wines from the Prince's cellars. When they had returned to Baidor, some of the wines were distributed amongst the men, and the remainder sent to headquarters at Sebastopol.

From Baidor they were removed to Balaklava, just in time to be present at the battle of Tchernaya, their position being behind the Sardinians, who had entered into an alliance with the British, and had sent out a small force to the Crimea. These allies fought well, and gave a good account of themselves in the struggle against the Russians. The 17th Lancers were there in case their services should be required.

It may here be stated that Sergeant-Major Nunnerley was present during the whole of the engagements; and he was never absent from one day's duty during the time he was in the Crimea, notwithstanding the numerous difficulties and hardships with which he had so frequently to contend. He was without boots or shoes most of the winter of 1854, and was obliged to tie the soles of his old shoes to his feet to keep them off the ground. In consequence of this his right foot was frost bitten, but had nearly recovered at the approach of milder weather. He still feels the effects of that winter in damp or wet weather, which causes him to keep fresh in his mind most of the incidents connected with the different battles. Balaklava is not without its incidents—amusing, and, in some cases, fatal. His mind often reflects upon the coolness of a man named Buck, of the same regiment, who, like himself, had his share of narrow escapes. Returning under a heavy fire, after the famous charge, a bullet passed through Buck's whiskers, and he immediately said, " I am shot;" but, putting his hand to his cheek, said, "No, I am not, but it is close shaving." When at Balaklava, one of the artillery-men dropped a bucket down a well, which he thought he could get by going down and putting his feet against the sides of the well in order to avoid a too quick and possibly fatal descent. He tried this experiment, but found out his mistake when too late, as the sides of the well, against which he thought to lean, gave way, and precipitated him to the bottom. Another man tried to rescue him, but got fast, and was with difficulty brought out of his dangerous position, leaving his comrade buried at the bottom. The well was afterwards filled up.

Respecting the Duke of Cambridge, Sergeant-Major Nunnerley states that His Royal Highness is one of the best officers that ever went into a battlefield, being both brave, and yet kind and humane; and his qualities for good drill and discipline cannot be excelled. A soldier's friend!—He has done more for the good and comfort of the Army than any other commander in his high and responsible position ever did. Before the battle of Inkerman took place, the escort that went with His Royal Highness and Lord Raglan to examine the position of the guns said, the Duke of Cambridge and Lord Raglan had had a few words about three guns in position below Inkerman Hill. His Royal Highness told the General (Lord Raglan) that there should have been at least twelve guns there instead of the three. Lord Raglan replied that three guns would be sufficient, as he thought the Russians would not attack that point. In a few days after, the Battle of Inkerman took place. The three guns, being in advance, were attacked by the Russians, and taken three times, but were as often retaken by the British. Had there been twelve guns in position, as suggested by His Royal Highness, the chance of the enemy to get on the top of Inkerman Hill would have been very doubtful.

When peace was proclaimed, the 17th Lancers were staying at Ismaid, in Turkey, where an order was given for all the soldiers who had been out on duty during the whole time of the campaign to parade in the square. Out of the 300 men of the 17th Lancers who left England, only 25 non-commissioned officers and men answered to the muster call, together with Adjutant Duncan, who was the only officer of the Regiment out during the whole of the time. All present were deeply affected at the loss of so many brave comrades,—a loss then too well verified by the small remnant of the regiment present to answer to the call! Such were some of the experiences of Sergeant-Major Nunnerley and the 17th Lancers, who, as English and British soldiers, had a fair and proud share in adding further victories and renown to the prestige of the British Army in the noble cause and mission of civilisation and national rights, for *Dieu défend le droit!*

With the survivors of his regiment, Sergeant-Major Nunnerley returned to Ireland, landing at Kingstown, and from thence he was sent to Limerick in command of a corporal and twelve men as letter-party to General Chatterton. When the garrison broke up, the regiment marched to Dublin, to be present at the grand banquet given to all soldiers who had returned from the Crimea. When the reduction of the army took place in 1857, Sergeant-Major Nunnerley left the service owing to not having received the just and reasonable reward he had duly merited during the eleven years he had served in the 17th Lancers and in the Crimean campaign.

On leaving the Army, Sergeant-Major Nunnerley obtained a situation as stationmaster at Disley, near Buxton; and when he had held that position for two years, he received a letter from the Right Hon. Lord Skelmersdale (now Earl of Lathom) stating his Lordship's intention of forming a Troop of Yeomanry Cavalry, and offering him the post of Drill Instructor to the Troop. He accepted the Office as Troop Sergeant-Major, and accordingly took up his residence at Ormskirk. In about a month the Troop was raised, forming the " D " Troop of the Lancashire Hussars, with Lord Skelmersdale as its first Captain. The Troop always made a good muster; and its efficiency and smart soldier-like appearance and mount have secured for the Troop the highest praise from the several Reviewing Officers and other competent judges of military discipline.

In consequence of illness, occasioned by drilling and his previous experiences in the Crimea, he found himself compelled to resign the office of Drill Instructor to the " D " Troop of Lancashire Hussars, which he did with great reluctance and no small amount of sincere regret, having to withdraw himself from intercourse with many friends and acquaintances whom he had learned to respect and honour as men and friends during the twenty-two years he had the privilege and pleasure of being connected with the Lancashire Hussars.—Sergeant-Major Nunnerley is now following the profession to which he was apprenticed.

———∘ₒ﹔ₒ∘○﹒——

Sergeant-Major Nunnerley has been awarded and decorated with the under-mentioned distinguished Medals, &c., which are now in his possession :—

> " CRIMEAN MEDAL," with Four Clasps.
>
> " TURKISH MEDAL," given by the Turkish Government.
>
> " FRENCH WAR MEDAL," and " DIPLOMA," for Services in the Field.

COPY OF DIPLOMAS.

FRENCH EMPIRE.
MILITARY MEDAL.

Mr. James Nunnerley, Sergeant of the 17th Regiment of Lancers, is informed that by Decree of the 6th March, 1861, made upon the proposal of the Minister, the Secretary of State to the War Department, the Emperor has conferred on him the Military Medal.

Intimation of this Decree is given to his Excellency, M., the High Chancellor of the Legion of Honour, who is charged to ensure the execution of it as that which concerns him.

Paris, 20th March, 1861.

The Marshal of France,

the Minister, the Secretary of State

to the War Department.

MILITARY MEDAL.

His Majesty the Emperor, by Decree of the 6th of March, one thousand eight hundred and sixty-one, has conferred the *Military Medal* on Mr. James Nunnerley, Sergeant of the 17th Regiment of Lancers. (English Army.)

Paris, 23rd March, 1861.

The High Chancellor,

of the Imperial Order of the Legion of Honour.

He has at various times received the following presents :—

Medal, with the following inscription :—" Presented to Mr. J. I. Nunnerley, by the inhabitants of Disley, as a token of their esteem towards him during the time he was in the employ of the London and North Western Railway Company, December, 1859."

Medal, &c., presented by the D Troop, L. H., July 20th, 1867. "This Medal, with a Purse, presented to Sergeant-Major Nunnerley, Lancashire Hussars, by the members of his Troop and a few friends."

Silver Snuff-Box, 19th May, 1873 :—" Presented to Sergeant-Major Nunnerley, by the Non-Commissioned Officers and Men of the D Troop, Lancashire Hussars."

Sword, presented to Sergeant-Major Nunnerley by the Non-Commissioned Officers and Men of the D Troop, Lancashire Hussars, May 15th, 1875.

Snuff-Box, bearing the following inscription:—" Presented to Sergeant-Major J. I. Nunnerley, together with Drawing-room Clock and Vases, and ' Tantalus ' Spirit Frame, on his retirement from the Lancashire Hussars, after twenty-two years' service, by the Right Hon. the Earl of Lathom, the Officers, and Non-Commissioned Officers of the D Troop, and a few friends, 18th October, 1881."

Extracts of Reports in "Ormskirk Advertiser" on the foregoing Presentations.

"THE LANCASHIRE HUSSARS, D TROOP.
"INTERESTING PRESENTATION."

"After upwards of twenty-two years' service in connection with the Lancashire Hussars, Sergeant-Major Nunnerley has resigned his position in the D Troop, and the day of the annual dinner was considered a very appropriate time for presenting him with some token of the esteem in which he was held by the officers and men of the troop. On Tuesday a fair number of men assembled at Lathom House. Having 'fell in' in the stable yard, the troop was put through a short drill, and marched to the front of the hall, where the Earl and Countess of Lathom and family and Colonel Macdonald (late of the 71st Highlanders) awaited them. The Earl of Lathom having inspected the men, his Lordship called Mr. Nunnerley to him, and said he had been requested by the men of the D Troop to make a presentation to him on the occasion of his retirement from the detachment. On their part and his own he had to thank him for the great attention and trouble he had taken with the troop since the first day it was formed, which was now upwards of twenty-one years ago. It was entirely owing to the time and care and trouble he had taken in the drill of the men, that they stood in such a high position, for he had been commended year after year by the inspecting officers on their fine appearance, and not a year had passed but the D troop had had the greatest praise of any in the regiment. He thanked him for the manner in which he had done his duty, and he thanked those men who had been in the troop from the time it was raised for having set such a good example to others. He had never had the slightest difficulty in filling up a vacancy, and that it would continue under the new Sergeant-Major he had no doubt, and that the men would bring the same commendation on the troop as it had hitherto received. In the names of the officers, the non-commissioned officers, and men of the troop, and of a few friends, he had great pleasure in handing the present to Sergeant-Major Nunnerley.—Sergeant-Major Nunnerley, in reply, said he was very pleased with the magnificent presents they had made him that day, and he was much obliged for them. It was very gratifying to him to receive them from his lordship, whom he had served as Sergeant-Major for upwards of twenty-two years, and from whom he had received many kindnesses. At the same time he would take the opportunity of thanking his lordship for the horse and trap he had so kindly given him. He again thanked all for the very handsome presents.—The Countess of Lathom then shook Sergeant-Major Nunnerley by the hand, and wished him health to enjoy them.—His lordship said this did not mean that Sergeant-Major Nunnerley was going to leave them altogether, for he hoped they would see him sometimes, whereupon the Sergeant-Major said he would always be glad to assist them in any way he could.

"THE LANCASHIRE HUSSARS.
"ANNUAL DINNER.—PRESENTATION TO SERGEANT-MAJOR NUNNERLEY.

"The Vice-Chairman (Sergeant Lycett) then rose and proposed the health of the Chairman (Sergeant-Major Nunnerley), and addressing Sergeant-Major Nunnerley, said—Having been formally appointed by my fellow comrades and friends to make our little presentation to you this evening, I feel highly honoured in rising to discharge a duty so pleasing to myself and so interesting to all present. In presenting you with this silver medal and purse and contents, we are, in a feeble manner, but nevertheless sincerely, giving expression to our admiration of your many private virtues, and of our appreciation of your public worth as a soldier and a gentleman. In our past intercourse with you as a soldier we have always found in you those qualifications which are eminently calculated to maintain the honour of England's defenders, and the high prestige of our beloved country; and we hope you may be spared for many years to exemplify, as heretofore, those qualities which have gained our esteem and admiration. I now beg, on behalf of the contributors, that you will be pleased to accept this medal and purse, with which we have to combine our best wishes for your future happiness as a faint expression of our esteem, and as a memento of a friendship that will ever be associated with reminiscences of the pleasantest character.—(Much cheering and cries of 'Hear, hear,' from the whole company followed the sergeant's concluding remarks.)—Mr. J. B. Lambert then stepped forward and placed the medal on the Sergeant-Major's left breast, and said he hoped the Sergeant-Major would live long to wear it.—The medal bore the following inscription :—'This medal, with purse, presented to Sergeant-Major Nunnerley, of the D troop of the Lancashire Hussars, by the members of his troop and a few friends. July, 1867.'—The Chairman then rose and said—Sergeant Lycett, brother comrades, and gentlemen,—I can hardly find words to express myself for the kind present you this day have given me. I shall wear the medal with great pleasure, and when I look upon it I shall think of the dear old comrades and friends who have so kindly presented me with it. Also for the purse I thank you most sincerely. Respecting the medal, you could not have given me anything I could prize more. I hope I may live long to wear it amongst you. Again, I thank you from the bottom of my heart, and conclude by heartily drinking the health of yourselves, your wives, and children, not forgetting your dear old parents.—The Chairman resumed his seat amid loud cheering.

"THE LANCASHIRE HUSSARS.

"Presentation to Sergeant-Major Nunnerley.

"On Monday, the D troop (Lord Skelmersdale's) assembled at Lathom House, when Sergeant-Major Nunnerley was presented with a handsome chased silver snuff box, bearing the following inscription :—'Presented to Sergeant-Major Nunnerley, by the non-commissioned officers and men of the D troop of Lancashire Hussars, 16th May, 1873.'

"The troop having been drawn up,

"Sergeant Sherlock advanced to the front, and said—Sergeant-Major Nunnerley, I have been requested by the non-commissioned officers and men of the D troop to present you with a small token of respect and esteem, and I assure you that I feel proud of being the medium of making this present to one whom I believe to be so deserving of it. It is not an article of very great value, but I am sure you will not regard it for its intrinsic worth, but look upon it, as it is intended, as a proof of the good wishes and confidence of those who receive instructions from you, which make our military duties quite a pleasure. Sergeant-Major Nunnerley, I may say that your persevering determination to make every man who joins the D troop thoroughly acquainted with his duties, and the gentlemanly way in which you impart those instructions, and your general conduct in connection with the troop, has gained for you the affection of the men, and the respect and esteem of all with whom you come in contact. Allow me, in the name of the non-commissioned officers and men, to present you with this token, and I hope you may long remain the Sergeant-Major of the D troop.

"Sergeant-Major Nunnerley in responding said—Brother comrades all—I return you my most sincere thanks for making me this most magnificent present to-day. When I look upon it I shall always remember those who gave me this beautiful silver box. I have always done my best to give satisfaction to the troop to which I belong. This is not the first presentation that has been made to me on similar occasions to this. I assure you that I am proud to belong to a troop of which Lord Skelmersdale is the noble captain, and I hope that I may be spared to live many years amongst you. It was my hobby to be a soldier from my youth, and as a soldier I have always tried to do my duty. I assure you I cannot express my feelings on this occasion as I should wish to do, so I will conclude by again expressing to you, Sergeant Sherlock, and comrades, my sincere thanks."

"THE LANCASHIRE HUSSARS.

"THE REVIEW.

" As the D troop assembled this morning, at the corner of Bath-street, it was apparent to all observers that something extraordinary was about to take place. At ten a large number had congregated, and the crowd continued swelling for a quarter of an hour afterwards. Of course, when anything beyond the routine of military life is to occur, little whispers are heard amongst the men, and this was the case this morning. We fortunately overheard that a presentation was to be made to Sergeant-Major Nunnerley, of the D troop (Lord Skelmersdale's.) Beyond the fact of the Sergeant-Major having been one who took part in the ' Charge of the Light Brigade,' he is bound to us by ties of pure friendship, he having, during the many years we have known him, shown us the greatest kindness and courtesy. The sword, which was presented to him by Sergeant Sherlock, is a well-made regulation one, and the event showed the high esteem in which Sergeant-Major Nunnerley is held by the men under his charge.

" Sergeant Sherlock said—Sergeant-Major Nunnerley, I wish to present you with this sword on behalf of the non-commissioned officers and the men of the D troop of the Lancashire Hussars, which is given to you for your kind, gentlemanly, and courteous conduct to us, and for the interest you take in us when we are assembled together. I feel proud in being requested to make this presentation, for I am sure you well deserve it. If ever you are required to draw it you will find it a good and trusty blade. Sergeant Sherlock then handed the sword to Sergeant-Major Nunnerley.

" The sword bore the following inscription :—

Presented to
SERGEANT-MAJOR NUNNERLEY,
By the Non-commissioned Officers and men of the
D Troop, Lancashire Hussars,
13th May, 1876.

"Sergeant-Major Nunnerley, in accepting the sword, said—Sergeant Sherlock, non-commissioned officers and men of the D troop of the Lancashire Hussars, I am extremely obliged to you for your kindness in presenting me with this sword. It has been my pleasure and duty to do the best I could for the troop, and I may say that I have been praised by those in command. I again thank you for your kindness, but I wish to say that it is my duty to do the best I can, not only for the D troop, but for the whole regiment. (Hear, hear). I have been now 17 times with you to Southport, and I have always done my duty in such a way as to get high credit from Lord Gerard. (Cheers.) It is a pleasant thing for me to receive this sword, and if ever the day should come when I may be required to aid in defending Old England, I trust that the One above will bring me safely out, as He has done before. (Cheers)."

AFTER serving in the Army and Yeomanry for Thirty-three years, with the exception of a few days, and being Drill Instructor nearly the whole of that period, Sergeant-Major Nunnerley now receives the sum of One Shilling per day in the shape of a pension, namely, Eightpence from the Yeomanry, and Fourpence from the Army; consequently, as already stated, he has been obliged to return to his own trade for support; and he begs very gratefully to thank his numerous Friends and the Public generally of the surrounding neighbourhood of Ormskirk for their kind and very generous patronage during the time he has been in Business; and hopes by strict attention and civility to his Customers to merit a continuance of their favour and support.

27, MOOR STREET,
    ORMSKIRK.

BATTLES

IN WHICH

Sergeant=Major Nunnerley

WAS ENGAGED, VIZ. :—

Bulganack, September 19th, 1854.

Alma, September 20th, 1854.

Mc. Kenzie's Farm, September 25th, 1854.

Taking Balaklava Fort and Harbour, September 26th, 1854.

Balaklava Charge, October 25th, 1854.

Inkerman, November 5th, 1854.

Tchernaya River, August 16th, 1855.

Sebastopol—(The whole of the Seige and taking of)—September 8th, 1855.

Address to Her Most Gracious Majesty The Queen, from the Survivors of the Non-commissioned Officers and Privates who rode in the Charge of the Light Brigade at Balaklava, on the 25th October, 1854.

Extract from the MORNING POST, *20th June, 1887.*

"Amongst the many congratulatory addresses presented to the Queen, there are few more interesting than that which has been presented on behalf of the survivors of the famous charge of the Light Brigade at Balaklava. The presentation is in every way gratifying. The Address which is beautifully emblazoned on a vellum scroll, and enclosed in a morocco case, is as follows :—' To Her most Gracious Majesty the Queen : May it please your Majesty, we, the undersigned non-commissioned officers and privates, being the survivors of those who rode in the Charge of the Light Brigade at Balaklava on the 25th October, 1854, beg humbly to approach your Majesty with every feeling of loyalty and deep respect on the auspicious occasion of the Jubilee year of Your Most Gracious Majesty's Reign, and trust that, with other of Your Majesty's subjects, we may be allowed to offer our sincere and very respectful congratulations ; and we further pray that the Almighty God may, in his infinite wisdom, grant you many years of health and strength to reign over Your Majesty's loyal subjects and vast dominions.' Signed by twenty-four of the 4th Queen's Own Light Dragoons, eight of the 8th Royal Irish Hussars, twenty-eight of the 11th Prince Albert's Own Hussars, sixteen of the 13th Light Dragoons, and twenty-five of the 17th Lancers. There are in all 103 signatures, and of these survivors, forty-five were wounded in the charge, and eight were taken prisoners. Two of the men signed with the left hand, having lost the sword arm in the battle."

The following is a copy of Her Majesty's Most Gracious Reply.

WHITEHALL,

16th July, 1887.

SIR,

I have had the honour to lay before the Queen the loyal and dutiful Address of the Non-commissioned Officers and Privates who rode in the Charge of the Light Brigade at Balaklava. And I have to inform you that Her Majesty was pleased to receive the same most graciously, and to command me to signify Her Majesty's lively remembrance of the splendid action in which they took part, and Her interest in the gallant survivors.

I have the honour to be,

Sir,

Your obedient Servant,

(Signed) HENRY MATHEWS.

G. L. SMITH, ESQ.,
President of the Balaklava Commemoration Society.

Copies of Valentines referred to at the commencement of this Sketch.

~~~~~~~~~~~~~~~~~~

Extracted from the Journal of the British Archæological Association. These Valentines were exhibited by Dr. Kendrick, M.D., of Warrington, March 31st, 1873.

~~~~~~~~~~~~~~~~~~

The valentines are written on squares of foolscap-paper, varying in size from 12 to 13 inches, and are doubled up in a very complicated manner, most difficult to describe, and all that can be attempted is to indicate the poems as they meet the eye, as fold after fold is raised. The first specimen we take is folded in a square, and has on its front a great pink heart surrounded by red and blue rays, and enclosed in a circle; and in each corner is a line of poetry, making up this quatrain :—

> "To thee I write, sweet Turtle Dove;
> I've wrote a morral of my love.
> The powers of envy can't pretend
> To say I have false storys pen'd."

On the back of the square is another, but much smaller red heart, declaring :—

> "Dear love, this heart, which you behold,
> Will break when you these lines unfold :
> Even so my heart with love-sick pain
> Sore wounded is, and breaks in twain."

As we continue to unfold the sheet we read :—

> "My dearest dear and blest divine,
> I've pictured here your heart and mine;
> But Cupid with his fatal dart
> Hath wounded deep my tender heart,
> And hath betwixt us set a cross,
> Which makes me to lament my loss."

On the inside of the sheet is a rich display of hearts and roses, mingled, amid which are the sun, moon, and stars, a most diabolical-looking Cupid, with a bow, etc., accompanied by this affectionate effusion :—

> " You are the girl and only maid
> That hath my tender heart betray'd.
> Nor ever will my heart have ease
> Until our hearts are joined like these.
>
> If you refuse to be my wife
> It will bereave me of my life.
> Pale Death at last must stand my friend,
> And bring my sorrows to an end
> Of your true love, valentine, and friend.
>
> T. H., Feb. 14, 1785."

The second valentine is, like the foregoing, folded up in a square form in a very ingenious manner.   On lifting the first folds, two hearts, united at their broad ends, are exposed to view, and around them we read a quatrain varying but little from that inscribed on the specimen we have just examined :—

> " This heart, my dear, as you behold
> Will break as you these leaves unfold.
> Even so my heart with love-sick pain
> Sore wounded is and breaks in twain."

When the sheet is expanded, we find in the corners water-coloured drawings of good-sized doves and tulips; and in the field a great rhomb with a heart in each angle, and a larger one in the middle, surrounded by these pathetic lines :—

> " O virgin fair ! O nymph divine !
> My life, my love, my heart is thine.
> A heart I ad (sic) that once was free,
> But now's confin'd in chains by thee.
> My roving heart can never rest
> Till it finds room in your sweet breast.
> A lover true, a maid sincere,
> Is to be praised—a thing most rare.
> Perhaps you think I am too bold
> Because I have not store of gold ;
> For if I ad (sic) you should have part
> But as I ant (sic) you have my heart.
>
> When this you see, pray think of me, and bear me in your mind,
> I am not like the weathercock that changes to every wind.
>
> THOS. PRESTON."

The last of the three valentines is without pictorial embellishments, but the paper is cut out by hand, in a bold pattern, somewhat in the fashion of a stove veil, flowers in diota-pots and hearts being the motives of the design.   It is folded over and

over so as to form a triangle or "cocked hat," and within is
written the following :—

> " Some draw valentines by lot,
> And some draw them that they love not,
> But I draw you whom I love best
> And chuse you out amongst the rest.
> The ring is round that hath no end,
> And this I send to you, my friend ;
> And if you take it in good part,
> I shall be glad with all my heart.
> Excuse me now for being so bold,
> I should have wrote your name with gold ;
> But gold was scarce, as you may think,
> Which made me write your name with ink ;
> But if you do these lines refuse,
> The paper burn ; pray me excuse.
>
> THOS. GROOM,—ANN JEBB."

This valentine presents two points of special interest, one
being the distinct allusion which it makes to the ancient practice
of drawing valentines by lot : the other, that it seems to be the
germ of the perforated, beehive-shaped *applique* which, when
raised, displays beneath it a beautiful visage, or a Cupid, a heart
struck by a dart, or some other touching device.